American Government

State Governments

by Connor Stratton

FOCUS READERS.
PIONEER

www.focusreaders.com

Copyright © 2024 by Focus Readers®, Lake Elmo, MN 55042. All rights reserved. No part of this book may be reproduced or utilized in any form or by any means without written permission from the publisher.

Focus Readers is distributed by North Star Editions:
sales@northstareditions.com | 888-417-0195

Produced for Focus Readers by Red Line Editorial.

Photographs ©: Shutterstock Images, cover, 1, 7, 8, 11, 17, 18, 21 (bottom); iStockphoto, 4, 13, 21 (top left), 21 (top right); Joe Andrucyk/Maryland GovPics, 14

Library of Congress Cataloging-in-Publication Data
Names: Stratton, Connor, author.
Title: State governments / by Connor Stratton.
Description: Lake Elmo, MN : Focus Readers, [2024] | Series: American government | Includes bibliographical references and index. | Audience: Grades 2-3
Identifiers: LCCN 2023002936 (print) | LCCN 2023002937 (ebook) | ISBN 9781637395936 (hardcover) | ISBN 9781637396506 (paperback) | ISBN 9781637397633 (ebook pdf) | ISBN 9781637397077 (hosted ebook)
Subjects: LCSH: State governments--United States--Juvenile literature. | Local government--United States--Juvenile literature.
Classification: LCC JK2408 .S8638 2024 (print) | LCC JK2408 (ebook) | DDC 320.10973--dc23/eng/20230130
LC record available at https://lccn.loc.gov/2023002936
LC ebook record available at https://lccn.loc.gov/2023002937

Printed in the United States of America
Mankato, MN
082023

About the Author

Connor Stratton writes and edits nonfiction children's books. He lives in Minnesota.

Table of Contents

CHAPTER 1
State Roles 5

CHAPTER 2
State Lawmakers 9

A CLOSER LOOK
State to State 12

CHAPTER 3
Governors 15

CHAPTER 4
State Courts 19

Focus on State Governments • 22
Glossary • 23
To Learn More • 24
Index • 24

Chapter 1

State Roles

Each state has a **government**. State governments do many things. They set **taxes**. They build roads. States make their own laws. They have their own courts, too.

States are in charge of many things. They run schools. They have police. States help with businesses. They help during disasters. States also have power over cities and towns. They have power over **counties**, too.

States cannot make their own money. Only the United States can print money.

Chapter 2

State Lawmakers

State governments have three branches. One is called the legislative branch. Lawmakers are part of it. They write bills. A bill is a plan for a law.

Lawmakers can argue for a bill. They can argue against it. Then they vote on it. More than half must vote yes. Then the bill passes. It goes to the state's governor. She or he can sign the bill. Then it becomes a law.

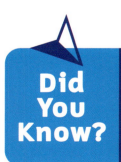

Did You Know? Most states have two **houses** of lawmakers. But Nebraska has only one house.

A Closer Look

State to State

Each state has different laws. **Licenses** are one example. People need licenses to drive. They must be old enough. But the age depends on the state. In some states, people can be 16 years old. In others, people must be at least 18.

Chapter 3

Governors

A governor leads each state. He or she runs one branch. It is the executive branch. It makes sure people follow state laws. The governor also works with lawmakers. He or she signs bills.

The governor has other roles, too. She or he helps with money. She or he chooses how to spend it. Each state also has armed forces. The governor leads them.

Did You Know? People pick governors. They pick lawmakers, too. People vote in **elections**.

Chapter 4

State Courts

States have courts. They form the third branch. It is the judicial branch. **Judges** run courts. They answer questions about laws.

A judge **rules** on a **case**. But one side might disagree. They can **appeal**. The case goes to a higher court. One side can appeal again. The case goes to the highest court. That court usually makes the final ruling.

Did You Know? The highest court has a name. It is often called the state supreme court.

Branches of State Government

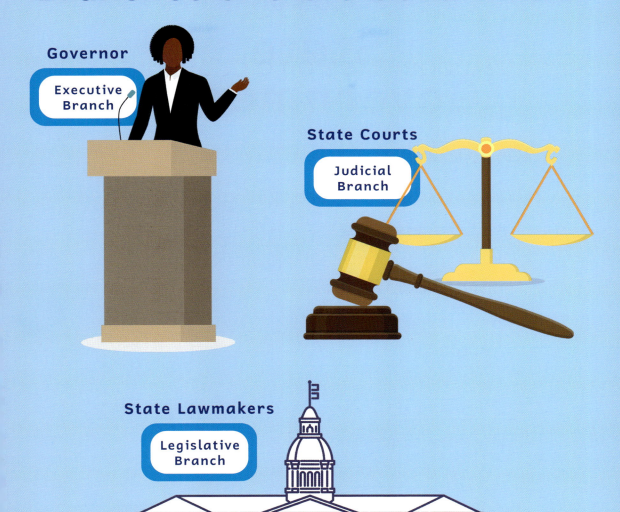

FOCUS ON
State Governments

Write your answers on a separate piece of paper.

1. Write a few sentences describing the three branches of state governments.

2. Would you want to meet a lawmaker in your state? Why or why not?

3. Who leads each state?
- **A.** court
- **B.** governor
- **C.** judge

4. Why does each state work differently?
- **A.** People do not vote for state leaders.
- **B.** States have all the same powers as the United States.
- **C.** States can make their own laws.

Answer key on page 24.

Glossary

appeal
To ask a higher court to review a case.

case
A problem people take to court for a decision on it.

counties
Areas in a state that have their own governments.

elections
When people vote for who they want in government jobs.

government
The people and groups that run a city, state, tribe, or country.

houses
Parts of the branch of government that makes laws.

judges
People who decide cases in courts of law.

licenses
Official permissions to do things.

rules
Makes a decision on a case.

taxes
Money people pay to their government.

To Learn More

BOOKS

Rustad, Martha E. H. *The State Governor*. North Mankato, MN: Capstone Press, 2020.

Ventura, Marne. *Government and Community*. Minneapolis: Abdo Publishing, 2019.

NOTE TO EDUCATORS

Visit **www.focusreaders.com** to find lesson plans, activities, links, and other resources related to this title.

Index

C
courts, 5, 19–21

E
elections, 16

G
governor, 10, 15–16, 21

L
lawmakers, 9–10, 15–16, 21

Answer Key: **1.** Answers will vary; **2.** Answers will vary; **3.** B; **4.** C